pancakes & waffles

By Lou Seibert Pappas

Photographs by Victoria Pearson

CHRONICLE BOOKS
SAN FRANCISCO

Library of Congress Cataloging-in-Publication Data:
Pappas, Lou Seibert.
  Pancakes & waffles / by Lou Seibert Pappas ;
photographs by Victoria Pearson.
    p. cm.
Includes index.
ISBN 0-8118-4551-6 (hardcover)
1. Pancakes, waffles, etc. I. Title: Pancakes & waffles. II.
Title.
TX770.P34P3623 2004
641.8'15—dc22
                2004001210

Manufactured in China.
Design and typesetting by Carole Goodman,
  Blue Anchor Design

Photographer's assistant: Jon Nakano
Prop stylist: Ann Johnstad
Prop stylist's assistant: Susan Robohm
Food stylist: Camille Renk
Food stylist's assistant: Gabriela Perez-Martinez

Distributed in Canada by Raincoast Books
9050 Shaughnessy Street
Vancouver, British Columbia V6P 6E5

10 9 8 7 6 5 4 3 2 1

Chronicle Books LLC
85 Second Street
San Francisco, California 94105

www.chroniclebooks.com

Grand Marnier is a registered trademark of
Marnier-Lapostolle; Sunset is a registered trademark of
Sunset Publishing Corporation.

DEDICATION

With love to a wonderful friend and superb taster, Ray S. Stewart.

TABLE OF CONTENTS

INTRODUCTION

THE CAPTIVATING AROMA OF HOT-OFF-THE-GRIDDLE PANCAKES OR freshly baked waffles is a tantalizing invitation for a sumptuous repast. Contemplate:

> Mom's Swedish rice cakes for a schoolday breakfast, a stack of sourdough hots at my uncle's sheep ranch, wild huckleberry pancakes at the Oregon coast Neskowin cabin, Dutch babies for an early *Sunset* magazine story, *fraises de bois*–smothered Belgian waffles in Brussels, buckwheat blini with osetra caviar in St. Petersburg, flaming Grand Marnier crêpes in Paris, and billowy Salzburger *nockerln* with food editors in Austria . . . for me, the memorable pancake and waffle menus pyramid through the years.

Pancakes and waffles are classed as pourable batter-style quick breads. Often they are almost identical in ingredients, with almost equal proportions of liquid and dry ingredients. These homey hot breads make a weekend breakfast a special occasion that becomes a lasting family tradition, memorable for all ages. Quick and easy to mix and bake, pancakes and waffles are certainly the good cook's friend. Besides being accessible for even beginning bakers to whip up in a flourish, they are also economical. Call them genies in the kitchen.

Plus, their versatility offers options for enhancing menus for various courses throughout the day. Waffles present a wholesome breakfast bread for simply topping with maple syrup. Pancakes offer a sumptuous brunch treat cloaked with fresh berries and sour cream. For luncheon or supper, both stand in as an entrée or an innovative appetizer for a party, and for a delectable dessert, a waffle-style ice cream sundae is divine.

The recipes in this book let the home cook be innovative with the wide variety of wholesome grains, nuts, and fresh and dried fruits that are available. Today's equipment is designed for complete satisfaction in the kitchen. Many utensils are nonstick on their surfaces. Yet other types of surfaces are now effective as well. The marketplace offers many styles of griddles, skillets, and electric waffle bakers in various sizes with decorative grids.

Over the centuries in America, these breads have gone in and out of fashion. With their popularity today, they are readily available in frozen food sections. Yet with their ease of preparation, it is more satisfying and healthful to bake them yourself.

Baking and savoring pancakes and waffles can be a joyful pastime as these easy recipes are designed for fun.

—*Lou Seibert Pappas*

PANCAKES

Ingredients

Pancake batters are simply based on flour, leavening, sweetening, a liquid such as milk or buttermilk, eggs, and melted butter or oil.

Though all-purpose flour is a staple, other flours and grains yield interesting flavors and healthful assets. Unbleached all-purpose flour has slightly more gluten than all-purpose flour and is used in some recipes. Whole-wheat pastry flour contributes a finer texture than all-purpose whole-wheat flour. Whole-wheat, rye, buckwheat, barley, oat, soy, semolina, and corn flours are easy to purchase in bulk bins for added enjoyment.

Baking powder and baking soda are used for leavening, although some-times yeast adds an extra boost as in sourdough pancakes. Granulated or brown sugar can be augmented or replaced by honey, maple syrup, or molasses.

Fresh fruit, including blueberries, strawberries, bananas, and dried cran-berries, cherries, or apricots, lend a sweet, juicy embellishment. A variety of nuts, wheat germ, and sesame seeds bring a toasty addition to tender cakes.

Unsalted butter uplifts the flavor, yet for healthful reasons canola oil, nut oil, or olive oil may substitute.

Techniques

Combine the dry ingredients in one bowl. Whisking is an easy method to mix dry ingredients, or use a spatula. It is not necessary to sift the flour in advance, but make certain there are no lumps in the baking powder or baking soda. If there are, mash them with a spoon before adding. If the egg or eggs are separated, beat the whites first until soft, glossy peaks form. Then with the beater or a whisk, combine the egg yolks, milk, and other moist ingredients. Pour the wet ingredients into the dry mixture and stir with a spatula or spoon with a quick, light hand just until combined. Fold in the beaten egg whites. Do not overmix, as a few streaks of egg white or lumps are fine. Because all cooks measure differently, sometimes the batter needs adjustment. If the batter appears too thick, thin it with a tablespoon or two of milk or buttermilk. If it seems too runny or thin, stir in a tablespoon or two of flour.

Equipment

A flat griddle is ideal, but a 12-inch skillet or electric skillet works well. Certain recipes call for specialty pans, such as a steel crêpe pan, yet an omelet pan can substitute. Use a small, deep bowl as directed for beating 2 eggwhites, otherwise a medium bowl works well for combining ingredients (unless otherwise specified).

Cooking

Seasoned pans need very little greasing. Wipe the pan with a butter wrapper, oil lightly, or use a nonstick spray. Heat the pan over medium heat until a few drops of water sizzle when dropped on the surface.

Pour the batter from a spoon, a ladle, or $\frac{1}{4}$-cup measure from a height of 2 to 3 inches above the pan to make even, round pancakes. Allow an inch of space between each one. Cook them about 2 minutes, check the underside, and if golden brown and bubbles appear on the surface, turn the pancakes over and cook the other side. (Note: A few types of pancakes do not form bubbles.) It will take about half the time for the second side to brown lightly, slightly less in color than the first side. Immediately transfer to warm plates or place on a baking sheet and keep warm in a 200°F oven while you cook the remaining batter. It is not necessary to grease the pan between batches of pancakes.

Freezing and Reheating

Extra pancakes can be frozen in airtight lock-top plastic bags. Reheat in a toaster oven or a regular oven at 350°F for 8 to 10 minutes. A microwave tends to toughen pancakes.

WAFFLES

Equipment

When electric irons were created in the twentieth century, waffle suppers came into vogue, featuring a variety of creamed chicken and tuna sauces as toppings. Electric waffle irons are available in many shapes and sizes with various designs in the grids. Some are round, oblong, or square with heart-shaped or animal designs. The Belgian waffle iron is characterized by extra-deep grids. The testing of these recipes was done in a 7-inch round waffle iron and an oblong $4\frac{1}{2}$-by-9-inch Belgian waffle iron.

It is essential to properly season a waffle iron following the manufacturer's instructions unless it is a nonstick model. If you lack seasoning information, follow this procedure: Preheat the iron on medium-high. Open the lid and brush the surface lightly with vegetable oil. Close the lid and heat just until steaming. Open the lid, wipe the surface, and let cool.

Never immerse an iron in water, wash it with soap, or use a scouring pad on the surface. It may be brushed with a kitchen brush, or a clean old toothbrush is a handy tool. An iron treated in this way should not need greasing between bakings.

Baking Waffles

Preheat the waffle iron on medium until the indicator light shuts off or signifies it is ready. Pour in enough batter, about 1 cup, to cover at least two-thirds of the surface. The amount will vary with the size of your waffle iron and the recipe. The batter should flow and make a complete, full-sized waffle. Gently close the lid. Let cook about 4 minutes or until the steam stops. Gently lift the lid, and if it refuses to open, close the iron and cook 1 minute longer. Then open the lid—it should release easily—and check for a rich brown color and crisp crust. If it meets these criteria, remove the waffle with a fork to a warm plate. Or place it on a baking sheet and keep warm in a 200°F oven.

After baking the first waffle, you may need to adjust the thermostat. A higher temperature creates a crisp waffle, while a lower temperature results in a moister, tender waffle.

Freezing and Reheating

Because reheated waffles taste freshly made, it is handy to bake all the batter at one time and have the bonus of extra waffles for later enjoyment. Waffles freeze beautifully. Let them cool completely, slip into a lock-top plastic bag, and freeze for up to 2 months. Reheat (without thawing) in a toaster or toaster oven until hot through and crisp, or in a preheated 350°F oven for 10 minutes.

Note: These recipes were tested with whole milk, large eggs, and unsalted butter or canola or olive oil. There is little difference if you substitute low-fat or 1% milk.

PERFECT
PANCAKES

PANCAKES HAVE EVOLVED INTO A SOPHISTICATED STAPLE

from their origin centuries ago as a symbol of the Christian Eucharistic wafer. They have had an illustrious history as different countries developed their own specialties. Shrove pancakes have been savored throughout Europe since the Middle Ages. Native Americans introduced Colonial settlers to maize cakes. They cooked these pancakes and others made with various wheat-free flours over an open hearth on a bakestone.

In fact, cultures throughout the world all feature variations of the pancake. French crêpes, Russian *blini,* Austrian *nockerli,* Scottish oatcakes, and German billowy oven pancakes have been cherished for centuries. All of these specialties are delightful to savor for an easy-to-cook wholesome treat throughout the day.

In modern America, pancakes have long been a favorite breakfast staple. Whether they are called hotcakes, griddle cakes, flannel cakes, flapjacks, or johnnycakes, these soft-crusted cartwheels with a spongy center are designed to soak up a luscious syrup or cushion a sweet or savory topping for a delectable weekend brunch or hearty daily fare.

Classic Buttermilk Pancakes

Credit buttermilk and beaten egg whites for turning out these particularly light and special pancakes. It is hard to surpass this longtime favorite duo for griddle cakes. This versatile batter can be varied with countless flavor variations.

2 cups all-purpose flour

2 teaspoons sugar

1 teaspoon baking powder

1 teaspoon baking soda

¼ teaspoon salt

2 large eggs, separated

2 cups plus 2 tablespoons buttermilk

2 tablespoons unsalted butter, melted, or canola oil, plus extra for greasing

Butter and maple syrup, Swiss Whipped Honey Butter (page 74) or Maple Sugar–Pecan Butter (page 74) for topping

In a bowl, combine the flour, sugar, baking powder, baking soda, and salt. In a small, deep bowl, beat the egg whites with an electric mixer until soft, glossy peaks form. In another bowl, beat or whisk together the egg yolks, buttermilk, and butter. Add the buttermilk mixture to the dry ingredients and mix just until combined. Fold in the egg whites.

Heat a griddle or large skillet over medium heat and grease lightly. For each pancake, spoon or pour about ¼ cup batter onto the hot griddle. Cook until bubbles appear on the surface and the edges look dry, about 2 minutes. Turn over and cook until golden brown, about 1 minute more. Serve immediately or transfer pancakes to a baking sheet and keep warm in a 200°F oven. Bake the remaining batter as directed. Top with butter and maple syrup, Swiss Whipped Honey Butter, or Maple Sugar–Pecan Butter.

MAKES ABOUT FOURTEEN 4-INCH PANCAKES; SERVES 4

Variations:

Cranberry-Pecan Pancakes: Add ⅔ cup dried cranberries, ⅔ cup toasted chopped pecans, 1 teaspoon ground cinnamon, and 4 teaspoons grated orange zest to the batter.

Blueberry Pancakes: Add 1½ cups fresh or frozen blueberries, 3 tablespoons packed light brown sugar, and 1 teaspoon ground cinnamon to the batter.

Strawberry Pancakes: Add 1½ cups fresh or frozen sliced strawberries and 3 tablespoons sugar to the batter.

Blueberry-Cornmeal Pancakes

These pancakes bake on a film of wheat germ for a toasty finish. If blue cornmeal is available, it intensifies the bluish hue of the pancakes.

1½ cups unbleached all-purpose flour

½ cup yellow, white, or blue cornmeal

2 teaspoons baking powder

1 teaspoon ground cinnamon

½ teaspoon baking soda

¼ teaspoon salt

2 large eggs, separated

1½ cups buttermilk

½ cup milk

4 tablespoons (½ stick) unsalted butter, melted, plus extra for greasing

2 tablespoons maple syrup

1½ cups fresh or frozen blueberries

About ½ cup wheat germ

Maple syrup, Swiss Whipped Honey Butter (page 74), or Maple Sugar–Pecan Butter (page 74) for topping

In a bowl, combine the flour, cornmeal, baking powder, cinnamon, baking soda, and salt. In a small, deep bowl, beat the egg whites with an electric mixer until soft, glossy peaks form. In another bowl, beat or whisk together the egg yolks, buttermilk, milk, butter, and maple syrup. Add the buttermilk mixture to the dry ingredients and mix just until combined. Fold in the egg whites and blueberries.

Heat a griddle or large skillet over medium heat and grease lightly. Scatter 2 tablespoons of wheat germ over the surface. For each pancake, spoon or pour about ¼ cup batter onto the hot griddle. Cook until bubbles appear on the surface and the edges look dry, about 2 minutes. Turn over and cook until golden brown, about 1 minute more. Repeat coating the pan with wheat germ for the remaining batter. Serve immediately or transfer pancakes to a baking sheet and keep warm in a 200°F oven. Garnish with butter and maple syrup, Swiss Whipped Honey Butter, or Maple Sugar–Pecan Butter.

MAKES ABOUT SIXTEEN 4-INCH PANCAKES; SERVES 4

Four-Grain Fitness Pancakes

Vary these healthful pancakes with the grains at hand. Toss in some toasted sesame seeds or toasted chopped walnuts, pecans, or almonds for a quick crunchy addition.

½ cup all-purpose flour

½ cup whole-wheat flour

½ cup rye flour

½ cup barley or buckwheat flour

¼ cup cornmeal

¼ cup toasted wheat germ

2 teaspoons baking powder

1 teaspoon ground cardamom

½ teaspoon baking soda

¼ teaspoon salt

2 large eggs, separated

1½ cups buttermilk

½ cup milk

¼ cup canola oil, plus extra for greasing

2 tablespoons honey or maple syrup

Plain yogurt for topping

Fresh sliced nectarines, blueberries, or blackberries, or Sugar-Free Apple Spread (page 78) for topping

In a bowl, whisk together the flours, cornmeal, wheat germ, baking powder, cardamom, baking soda, and salt. In a small, deep bowl, beat the egg whites with an electric mixer until soft, glossy peaks form. In another bowl, beat or whisk together the egg yolks, buttermilk, milk, oil, and honey. Pour the buttermilk mixture into the dry ingredients and mix just until combined. Fold in the egg whites.

Heat a griddle or large skillet over medium heat and grease lightly. For each pancake, spoon or pour about ¼ cup batter onto the hot griddle. Cook until bubbles appear on the surface and the edges look dry, about 2 minutes. Turn over and cook until golden brown, about 1 minute more. Serve immediately or transfer pancakes to a baking sheet and keep warm in a 200°F oven. Bake the remaining batter as directed. Top with yogurt and fruit or Sugar-Free Apple Spread.

MAKES ABOUT FOURTEEN 4-INCH PANCAKES; SERVES 4

Buckwheat Pancakes with Chèvre, Salmon, and Dill

Serve these savory pancakes for an elegant brunch or late supper. Use soft chèvre (goat cheese) for a snowy white color contrast with the coral salmon and fresh dill.

1⅓ cups unbleached all-purpose flour

⅔ cup buckwheat flour

1 tablespoon packed light brown sugar

2 teaspoons baking powder

2 teaspoons ground cardamom

½ teaspoon baking soda

¼ teaspoon salt

2 large eggs, separated

1½ cups buttermilk

½ cup milk

4 tablespoons (½ stick) unsalted butter, melted, or canola oil, plus extra for greasing

2 tablespoons molasses

4 ounces chèvre

4 ounces smoked salmon

2 tablespoons chopped fresh dill

In a bowl, whisk together the flours, sugar, baking powder, cardamom, baking soda, and salt. In a small, deep bowl, beat the egg whites with an electric mixer until soft, glossy peaks form. In another bowl, beat or whisk together the egg yolks, buttermilk, milk, butter, and molasses. Add the buttermilk mixture to the dry ingredients and mix just until combined. Fold in the egg whites.

Heat a griddle or large skillet over medium heat and grease lightly. For each pancake, spoon or pour about 3 tablespoons batter onto the hot griddle. Cook until bubbles appear on the surface and the edges look dry, about 2 minutes. Turn over and cook until golden brown, about 1 minute more. Serve immediately or transfer pancakes to a baking sheet and keep warm in a 200°F oven. Bake the remaining batter as directed. Serve garnished with chèvre, smoked salmon, and dill.

MAKES ABOUT EIGHTEEN 3-INCH PANCAKES; SERVES 6

Granola-Yogurt Pancakes

Your favorite granola lends a crunchy bite and healthful goodness to these tender pancakes. Any extra pancakes can be frozen. They reheat quickly over medium heat in a skillet or in the oven (see page 9).

1½ cups granola

1 cup unbleached all-purpose flour

½ cup whole-wheat flour

¼ cup packed light brown sugar

1½ teaspoons baking powder

1 teaspoon ground cinnamon

½ teaspoon baking soda

¼ teaspoon salt

2 cups plain yogurt

2 large eggs

¼ cup canola or nut oil, plus extra for greasing

Homemade Maple Syrup (page 73) or Swiss Whipped Honey Butter (page 74) for topping

In a bowl, combine the granola, flours, sugar, baking powder, cinnamon, baking soda, and salt. In another bowl, beat or whisk together the yogurt, eggs, and oil. Add the yogurt mixture to the dry ingredients and mix just until combined.

Heat a griddle or large skillet over medium heat and grease lightly. For each pancake, spoon or pour about ¼ cup batter onto the hot griddle. Cook until bubbles appear on the surface and the edges look dry, about 2 minutes. Turn over and cook until golden brown, about 1 minute more. Serve immediately or transfer pancakes to a baking sheet and keep warm in a 200°F oven. Bake remaining batter as directed. Top with Homemade Maple Syrup or Swiss Whipped Honey Butter.

MAKES ABOUT SIXTEEN 4-INCH PANCAKES; SERVES 4

Variation:
Cherry-Almond Pancakes: In place of the granola add ½ cup dried cherries or golden raisins, ½ cup toasted chopped almonds, and 4 teaspoons grated orange zest to the batter.

Triple Ginger Pancakes

Ginger in three styles—fresh, ground, and crystallized—imparts a lively pow and uplift to these spicy pancakes. Serve them at an intimate brunch with sautéed apple slices or accompany with a fresh fruit salad of diced pineapple, kiwi fruit, and mango and drizzle with maple syrup. Whole-wheat pastry flour lends a finer texture than standard whole-wheat flour.

1½ cups unbleached or regular all-purpose flour

½ cup whole-wheat pastry flour

⅓ cup packed light brown sugar

1 tablespoon baking powder

2 teaspoons ground ginger

1 teaspoon ground cinnamon

½ teaspoon ground cloves

½ teaspoon baking soda

¼ teaspoon salt

2 large eggs, separated

2 cups milk

⅓ cup molasses

5 tablespoons unsalted butter, melted, or canola oil, plus extra for greasing

2 tablespoons fresh grated ginger

½ cup chopped crystallized ginger

Sautéed Cinnamon Apple Slices (page 83), Almond-Honey Butter (page 75), or Rum Hard Sauce (page 92) for topping

In a bowl, combine the flours, sugar, baking powder, ground ginger, cinnamon, cloves, baking soda, and salt. In a small, deep bowl, beat the egg whites with an electric mixer until soft, glossy peaks form. In another bowl, beat or whisk together the egg yolks, milk, molasses, butter, and fresh ginger. Add the milk mixture to the dry ingredients and mix just until combined. Fold in the egg whites and crystallized ginger.

Heat a griddle or large skillet over medium heat and grease lightly. For each pancake, spoon or pour about ¼ cup batter onto the hot griddle. Cook until bubbles appear on the surface and the edges look dry, about 2 minutes. Turn over and cook until golden brown, about 1 minute more. Serve immediately or transfer pancakes to a baking sheet and keep warm in a 200°F oven. Bake the remaining batter as directed. Top with Sautéed Cinnamon Apple Slices, Almond-Honey Butter, or Rum Hard Sauce.

MAKES ABOUT SIXTEEN 4-INCH PANCAKES; SERVES 4

Swedish Cinnamon-Rice Cakes

These custard-like creamy pancakes are excellent topped with blackberries or raspberries or berry syrup. They were a childhood favorite of mine and often were dolloped with wild blackberry or sour cherry preserves. The easy double boiler method of cooking the rice creates a soft homogeneous consistency rather than individual grains of rice that you would achieve by the stove-top method.

2 cups milk

⅓ cup uncooked long-grain white rice

1 tablespoon honey

Dash of salt

3 large eggs

½ teaspoon ground cinnamon

Dash of freshly grated nutmeg

Unsalted butter or canola oil for greasing

Fresh blackberries or raspberries, Blueberry Sauce (page 79), berry syrup, or preserves for topping

In the top of a double boiler over simmering water, combine the milk, rice, honey, and salt. Cover and cook, stirring occasionally, for 1½ hours or until the milk is absorbed and the rice is creamy. Let cool to room temperature 30 to 40 minutes. In a bowl, beat the eggs and mix in the cinnamon, nutmeg, and rice mixture.

Heat a griddle or large skillet over medium heat and grease lightly. For each pancake, spoon about 2 tablespoons batter onto the hot griddle. Cook slowly until golden brown underneath, about 2 minutes. Turn over and cook about 1 minute more. Serve immediately or transfer pancakes to a baking sheet and keep warm in a 200°F oven. Bake the remaining batter as directed. Top with fruit, syrup, or preserves.

MAKES ABOUT TWENTY 3-INCH PANCAKES; SERVES 4

Ricotta Soufflé Pancakes with Raspberries

Delicate, soufflé-like cheese pancakes are a treat for brunch or dessert topped with raspberry sauce, a few raspberries, and crème fraîche. They may be made an hour in advance and reheated, as they retain their puff nicely. As an option for a first course or luncheon entrée, reduce the sugar to 1 tablespoon and top with smoked salmon, crème fraîche, and minced dill.

4 large eggs, separated

2 tablespoons sugar

1 cup ricotta cheese

⅓ cup all-purpose flour

2 tablespoons unsalted butter, melted, plus extra for greasing

2 teaspoons grated lemon zest

⅛ teaspoon salt

Raspberry-Framboise Sauce (page 82) for topping

½ cup fresh raspberries for topping

About ½ cup crème fraîche or Candied Ginger, Mango, and Lime Spread (page 77) for topping

In a bowl, beat the egg whites with an electric mixer until soft peaks form, then beat in the sugar until medium glossy peaks form. In another bowl, beat the egg yolks until thick and pale in color, then beat in the cheese, flour, butter, zest, and salt. Fold ¼ of the beaten egg whites into the yolk mixture to lighten, then fold in the remaining egg whites.

Heat a griddle or large skillet over medium heat and grease lightly. For each pancake, spoon about 3 large tablespoons batter onto the hot griddle. Cook slowly for about 1½ minutes until golden brown underneath, then turn the pancakes over and cook about 30 seconds longer. Bake the remaining batter as directed. Keep the pancakes warm in a 200°F oven for 10 to 15 minutes, until ready to serve.

For each serving, place 4 pancakes on a plate, drizzle with a little raspberry sauce and top with a few berries and a spoonful of crème fraîche or top with Candied Ginger, Mango, and Lime Spread.

MAKES ABOUT SIXTEEN 3½-INCH PANCAKES; SERVES 4

Cottage Cheese Pancakes with Blackberries and Sour Cream

These tender cheese pancakes are perfect with a shower of berries and a dollop of sour cream. They make a delightful companion to a fresh fruit salad for brunch or luncheon.

1 cup all-purpose flour

2 tablespoons sugar

1½ teaspoons baking powder

¼ teaspoon baking soda

¼ teaspoon freshly grated nutmeg

⅛ teaspoon salt

2 large eggs, separated

¾ cup small-curd cottage cheese

⅔ cup milk

2 tablespoons unsalted butter, melted, or canola oil, plus extra for greasing

2 tablespoons grated lemon zest

Fresh blackberries or raspberries for topping

Sour cream for topping

In a bowl, combine the flour, sugar, baking powder, baking soda, nutmeg, and salt. In a small, deep bowl, beat the egg whites with an electric mixer until soft, glossy peaks form. In another bowl, beat or whisk together the egg yolks, cottage cheese, milk, butter, and zest. Add the cottage cheese mixture to the dry ingredients and mix just until combined. Fold in the egg whites.

Heat a griddle or large skillet over medium heat and grease lightly. For each pancake, spoon about 3 tablespoons batter onto the hot griddle. Cook until bubbles appear on the surface and the edges look dry, about 2 minutes. Turn over and cook until golden brown, about 1 minute more. Serve immediately or transfer pancakes to a baking sheet and keep warm in a 200°F oven. Bake the remaining batter as directed. Top with berries and sour cream.

MAKES ABOUT TWENTY 3-INCH PANCAKES; SERVES 4

Dutch Baby with Berries and Sour Cream

This billowy pancake has a German origin, yet the name originated when a popular Seattle restaurant named Manka's made miniature pancakes and the owner's children dubbed them Dutch Babies. This spectacular pancake is surprisingly easy to turn out and makes a stunning presentation at the table. Top the pancake with mixed berries, sour cream or yogurt, and a shower of raw sugar. Fresh sliced kiwi fruit, nectarines, or peaches are delicious cloaking it as well.

2 tablespoons unsalted butter or canola oil

¾ cup milk

¾ cup all-purpose flour

3 large eggs

2 tablespoons honey

1 teaspoon vanilla extract

⅛ teaspoon salt

2 tablespoons grated lemon zest

Confectioners' sugar for dusting

2 cups fresh mixed raspberries, blueberries, and sliced strawberries for topping

½ cup sour cream or plain yogurt for topping

2 tablespoons raw sugar for topping

Preheat the oven to 425°F. Place the butter in a 12-inch ovenproof skillet and heat in the oven for 10 minutes.

In a bowl, combine the milk, flour, eggs, honey, vanilla, salt, and zest and whisk until smooth. Pour into the hot pan, return to the oven, and bake for 20 to 25 minutes or until puffy and golden brown on the edges. Remove from the oven and dust with confectioners' sugar. Cut in wedges and top with berries, sour cream or yogurt, and raw sugar.

SERVES 4

Apple-Oatmeal Pancakes

Tart diced apples and apple juice punctuate these wholesome low-fat breakfast cakes for a tasty takeoff on Scottish oatcakes. A handful of dried cranberries or cherries lends a tart-sweet accent.

2 cups apple juice

1⅓ cups rolled oats

½ cup wheat germ

2 cups all-purpose flour

1 tablespoon baking powder

1 teaspoon ground cinnamon

½ teaspoon baking soda

¼ teaspoon salt

1 cup buttermilk or plain yogurt

¼ cup maple syrup

4 tablespoons (½ stick) unsalted butter, melted, or nut oil, plus extra for greasing

2 large eggs

½ cup dried cranberries or dried cherries

2 large Granny Smith apples, peeled, cored, and diced

Butter and maple syrup, Swiss Whipped Honey Butter (page 74), Sugar-Free Apple Spread (page 78), or Maple Sugar–Pecan Butter (page 74) for topping

In a medium saucepan, heat the apple juice to boiling and pour over the oats and wheat germ in a bowl. Let stand 20 minutes.

In another bowl, combine the flour, baking powder, cinnamon, baking soda, and salt. In another bowl, beat or whisk together the buttermilk, maple syrup, butter, and eggs. Add the buttermilk mixture and cranberries to the dry ingredients and mix just until combined. Stir in the oatmeal and apples.

Heat a griddle or large skillet over medium heat and grease lightly. For each pancake, spoon about ¼ cup batter onto the hot griddle. Cook until golden brown underneath and the edges look dry, about 2 minutes. Turn over and cook until golden brown, about 1 minute more. Serve immediately or transfer pancakes to a baking sheet and keep warm in a 200°F oven. Bake the remaining batter as directed. Top with butter and maple syrup, Swiss Whipped Honey Butter, Sugar-Free Apple Spread, or Maple Sugar–Pecan Butter.

MAKES ABOUT TWENTY 4-INCH PANCAKES; SERVES 4 TO 6

Rolled Pancake Cartwheels

These plate-size egg pancakes are delicious and fast to roll. Dust each cartwheel with confectioners' sugar and a commercial red currant–raspberry spread or homemade apple butter or mango butter and roll into the shape of a long, thin cigar. Or dot the pancakes with raspberries and sour cream before rolling.

⅔ cup half-and-half or milk

4 large eggs

¼ cup unbleached all-purpose flour

4 teaspoons orange liqueur or orange juice concentrate

4 teaspoons grated lemon zest or orange zest

1 tablespoon sugar

Dash of salt

Unsalted butter as needed

Confectioners' sugar and red currant–raspberry spread, Swiss Whipped Honey Butter (page 74), Sugar-Free Apple Spread (page 78), or Candied Ginger, Mango, and Lime Spread (page 77) for topping

In a blender container, combine the half-and-half, eggs, flour, liqueur, zest, sugar, and salt; cover and blend just until smooth. Or place in a bowl and beat with a whisk.

Heat a large 10- or 12-inch skillet over medium heat and butter pan lightly. Pour in just enough batter to coat the pan, tilting the pan as you do so. Cook slowly until lightly browned underneath, about 2 minutes. Turn pancake over and brown the other side, about 1 minute more. Dust with confectioners' sugar and spread with red currant–raspberry spread, Swiss Whipped Honey Butter, Sugar-Free Apple Spread, or Candied Ginger, Mango, and Lime Spread and roll up tightly. Place on an ovenproof platter and keep warm in a 200°F oven. Repeat with the remaining batter, greasing the pan as needed.

MAKES 8 TO 10 PANCAKES; SERVES 3 TO 4

Blini with Sour Cream and Caviar

This traditional yeast-raised Russian pancake is cooked in neat appetizer portions. Top with sour cream and caviar for a chic party appetizer or a holiday gala celebration. Flutes of champagne make perfect sippers alongside.

¼ cup warm water

1½ teaspoons active dry yeast

½ teaspoon granulated sugar

¾ cup milk

½ cup unbleached all-purpose flour

½ cup buckwheat flour

1 tablespoon packed brown sugar

⅛ teaspoon salt

2 large eggs, separated

2 tablespoons unsalted butter, melted, or canola oil, plus extra for greasing

1 tablespoon molasses

⅓ cup sour cream for topping

1 ounce caviar for topping

2 tablespoons chopped fresh chives or dill for topping

In a small bowl, combine the water, yeast, and granulated sugar and let stand until foamy, 5 to 10 minutes. In a saucepan, heat the milk to lukewarm. In another bowl, combine the flours, brown sugar, and salt. Stir in the milk, egg yolks, butter, molasses, and yeast mixture, and beat well. Cover and let rise in a warm place until doubled in size, about 1½ hours.

In a small, deep bowl, beat the egg whites with an electric mixer until soft, glossy peaks form. Fold into the batter.

Heat a griddle or large skillet over medium heat and grease lightly. For each pancake, spoon or pour about 2 tablespoons batter onto the hot griddle. Cook until bubbles appear on the surface and the edges look dry, about 2 minutes. Turn over and cook until golden brown, about 30 seconds more. Transfer to a baking sheet and keep warm in a 200°F oven while baking the remaining batter. Serve topped with sour cream, caviar, and chopped fresh chives or dill.

MAKES ABOUT EIGHTEEN 2-INCH PANCAKES;
SERVES 6 TO 8 AS AN APPETIZER

Savory Vegetable Pancakes

A variety of colorful vegetables enriches these tender pancakes. They make a tasty accompaniment to chicken-apple sausages and fresh fruit for brunch or red snapper or pork chops for dinner.

3 tablespoons unsalted butter or canola oil

2 cups shredded vegetables, such as carrots, zucchini, yellow crookneck squash, brown cremini mushrooms, or white mushrooms

2 large egg yolks or 1 large egg

½ cup sour cream

3 tablespoons cornstarch

1 tablespoon minced fresh chives

¼ teaspoon salt

Freshly ground black pepper

Tapenade (page 86) for topping

In a large skillet, heat 2 tablespoons butter over medium heat. Add desired vegetables. Sauté 1 to 2 minutes or until crisp-tender, stirring constantly. Remove from heat. Cool slightly.

In a bowl, beat the egg yolks or egg and mix in the sour cream, cornstarch, chives, salt, and pepper to taste. Stir in the sautéed vegetables.

In a large skillet, heat the remaining 1 tablespoon butter over medium-high heat. Spoon about 3 tablespoons batter into 3-inch patties in the skillet. Cook until lightly browned underneath, about 2 minutes. Turn and brown the other side, about 1 minute more. Transfer to a baking sheet and keep warm in a 200°F oven while baking the remaining batter. Serve hot or make in advance and reheat in a 325°F oven for 10 to 15 minutes or in a microwave. Top with a spoonful of Tapenade.

MAKES ABOUT TEN 3-INCH PANCAKES;

SERVES 4 AS A SIDE DISH

Potato-Chive Pancakes

Salting the potatoes and squeezing out the moisture causes these pancakes to acquire a crispy surface when browned. These are delightful with roast pork tenderloin or mild Italian or other specialty sausages and cinnamon-spiced applesauce.

4 medium russet or baking potatoes (about 1½ pounds)	3 tablespoons unbleached all-purpose flour
½ teaspoon salt	2 large cloves garlic, minced
2 large eggs	Freshly ground black pepper
1 small onion, grated	Vegetable oil for frying
3 tablespoons minced fresh chives or parsley	Sour cream or plain yogurt and apple-sauce for topping

Peel and finely grate the potatoes. Place in a colander and toss with the salt. Let stand 10 minutes, then squeeze out the moisture. In a large bowl, beat the eggs and stir in the potatoes, onion, chives, flour, garlic, and pepper to taste. Mix well.

In a large skillet, heat 2 tablespoons oil over medium heat. For each pancake spoon 1 heaping tablespoon of batter onto the hot pan and pat down lightly. Cook until lightly browned underneath, about 4 minutes. Turn over and cook until crisp and golden, about 2 minutes more. Transfer to a baking sheet and keep warm in a 200°F oven as you cook the remaining batter. Serve hot topped with sour cream or yogurt and applesauce.

MAKES ABOUT TEN 4-INCH PANCAKES;
SERVES 4 TO 6 AS A SIDE DISH

Butternut Squash Pancakes

Fine-textured butternut squash lends a cushiony texture and subtle flavor to these golden orange-scented pancakes. Mate them with Italian sausages or grilled pork chops and sautéed Granny Smith apple slices or applesauce for a welcome dinner pairing. Canned pumpkin can substitute for fresh cooked squash since it is usually butternut squash.

1⅓ cups unbleached all-purpose flour

4 teaspoons grated orange zest

2 teaspoons baking powder

½ teaspoon baking soda

½ teaspoon freshly grated nutmeg

¼ teaspoon salt

2 cups mashed cooked butternut squash or pumpkin

1½ cups apple juice or milk

4 tablespoons (½ stick) unsalted butter, melted, plus extra for greasing

2 large eggs

Plain yogurt or sour cream and chopped fresh chives for topping (optional)

In a bowl, combine the flour, zest, baking powder, baking soda, nutmeg, and salt. In another bowl, beat or whisk together the squash, juice, butter, and eggs. Add the squash mixture to the dry ingredients and mix just until combined.

Heat a griddle or large skillet over medium heat and grease lightly. For each pancake, spoon 1 heaping tablespoon of batter onto the hot griddle. Cook until golden brown underneath, about 2 minutes. Turn over and cook until golden, about 1 minute more. Serve immediately or transfer pancakes to a baking sheet and keep warm in a 200°F oven. Bake the remaining batter as directed. Top with yogurt or sour cream and chopped chives, if using.

MAKES ABOUT TWELVE 4-INCH PANCAKES;

SERVES 4 AS A SIDE DISH

Sourdough Pancakes

Start these pancakes several days in advance so the starter will have a pleasant sour aroma and decisive flavor. Once made, the starter needs replenishing once every week or two to keep it alive.

SOURDOUGH STARTER
2 cups lukewarm water

1 tablespoon active dry yeast

1 tablespoon honey

2 cups all-purpose flour

½ teaspoon salt

PANCAKES
2 cups milk

2 cups unbleached all-purpose flour

½ cup sourdough starter

2 large eggs

2 tablespoons sugar

½ teaspoon salt

½ teaspoon baking soda

Butter or oil for greasing

Homemade Maple Syrup (page 73) or Almond-Honey Butter (page 75) for topping

To make the starter: Prepare the starter several days in advance. In a bowl, combine the water, yeast, and honey. Let stand until foamy, 5 to 10 minutes. Beat in flour and salt. Cover with cheesecloth and let stand in a warm spot (ideally about 80°F) for 3 to 4 days, stirring several times a day. It will rise and fall and become bubbly.

This recipe makes about 2½ cups of starter. Replenish the starter every week by stirring in ½ cup flour and ½ cup lukewarm water.

To make the pancakes: Combine the milk, flour, and starter in a large bowl. Mix until blended, cover, and let stand in a warm place 8 hours or overnight. Stir in the eggs, sugar, salt, and baking soda, mixing until smooth.

Heat a griddle or large skillet over medium heat and grease lightly. For each pancake, spoon or pour about ¼ cup batter onto the hot griddle. Cook until bubbles appear on the surface and the edges look dry, about 2 minutes. Turn over and cook until golden brown, about 1 minute more. Serve immediately or transfer pancakes to a baking sheet and keep warm in a 200°F oven. Bake the remaining batter as directed. Top with Homemade Maple Syrup or Almond-Honey Butter.

MAKES ABOUT SIXTEEN 4-INCH PANCAKES; SERVES 4

Banana-Pecan Pancakes

Sliced bananas polka-dot each pancake with a golden color and delectable sweetness, which calls for a splash of rich buttery sauce. Cornmeal lends a subtle crunch.

1¾ cups all-purpose flour

¼ cup cornmeal

1 tablespoon packed light brown sugar

2 teaspoons baking powder

½ teaspoon baking soda

¼ teaspoon salt

2 large eggs, separated

1½ cups buttermilk

½ cup milk

4 tablespoons (½ stick) unsalted butter, melted, plus extra for greasing

2 tablespoons grated orange zest

⅔ cup toasted chopped pecans or walnuts

2 large bananas, peeled and thinly sliced

Rum Hard Sauce (page 92) or Maple Sugar–Pecan Butter (page 74) for topping

In a bowl, combine the flour, cornmeal, sugar, baking powder, baking soda, and salt. In a small, deep bowl, beat the egg whites with an electric mixer until soft, glossy peaks form. In another bowl, beat or whisk together the egg yolks, buttermilk, milk, butter, and zest. Add the buttermilk mixture to the dry ingredients and mix just until combined. Fold in the egg whites and nuts.

Heat a large griddle or skillet over medium heat and grease lightly. For each pancake, spoon or pour about ¼ cup batter onto the hot griddle. Scatter 4 or 5 banana slices over the surface of each cake. Cook until bubbles appear on the surface and the edges look dry, about 2 minutes. Turn over and cook until golden brown, about 1 minute more. Serve immediately or transfer pancakes to a baking sheet and keep warm in a 200°F oven. Bake the remaining batter as directed. Top with Rum Hard Sauce or Maple Sugar–Pecan Butter.

MAKES ABOUT FOURTEEN 4-INCH PANCAKES; SERVES 4

WINNING
WAFFLES

FOR A COSSETING TREAT OF HOMEY COMFORT FOOD,

a waffle is hard to beat. With its honeycomb decorative motif, a fragrant, crispy waffle is ready-made to cushion a pool of maple syrup and drizzle of melted butter. Yet these neat breakfast breads offer countless options for dining pleasure throughout the day. With flavors both savory and sweet, they excel with a spectrum of toppings. Fruit butters and syrups, nut butters, fresh berries, sliced peaches and nectarines, tropical fruits, fruit salads, sour cream, yogurt, crème fraîche, whipped cream, ice cream, and chocolate and caramel sauces all transform the basic waffle into a gourmet treat. What's more, baking them is easy!

Waffle irons were probably first used in Germany in the thirteenth century as hinged cast-iron paddles with wooden handles. They were held over the embers of the hearth fire to cook religious wafers. These crisp wafers were adopted throughout Europe as the French *gaufres*, the German *waffeln*, the Swedish *krum kager*, and the Italian *pizzelle*. Stovetop, cast-iron tools create a more cookie-like product than an ethereal leavened bread, and thus their batters have different proportions.

Modern waffle batters are close cousins to pancake batters. The dry and wet ingredients for both are first mixed in separate bowls and combined with a minimum of strokes. Sometimes the egg whites are beaten separately to lighten the batter. Extra fat in a waffle batter tends to produce a crispy, tender product. The fat, whether butter or oil, also prevents the waffle from sticking to the grids.

Classic Buttermilk Waffles

These crispy, light waffles are the basis for several flavor variations with dried and fresh fruit and nuts. You may wish to experiment with toppings such as whipped cream, strawberries, and yummy walnuts.

2 cups unbleached all-purpose flour

2 teaspoons baking powder

½ teaspoon baking soda

¼ teaspoon salt

4 large eggs, separated

2 cups buttermilk

4 tablespoons (½ stick) unsalted butter, melted, or canola oil

Butter, sauce, or syrup for topping

Preheat a waffle iron. In a bowl, whisk together the flour, baking powder, baking soda, and salt. In another bowl, beat the egg whites with an electric mixer until soft, glossy peaks form. In another bowl, beat or whisk together the egg yolks, buttermilk, and butter. Add the buttermilk mixture to the dry ingredients and mix just until combined. Fold in the egg whites.

Spoon or pour about 1 cup batter onto the hot iron. Close the lid. Bake until the waffle is golden brown, about 4 minutes. Remove with a fork to a warm plate. Serve at once or keep warm on a baking sheet in a 200°F oven. Repeat with the remaining batter. Serve these with any flavored butter, berry sauce, or syrup.

MAKES 6 TO 8 WAFFLES; SERVES 6 TO 8

Variations:

Cherry-Orange Waffles: Add ⅔ cup dried cherries and 4 teaspoons grated orange zest to the batter.

Whole-Wheat Walnut Waffles: Substitute 1 cup whole-wheat pastry flour or all-purpose whole-wheat flour for the all-purpose flour and add ⅔ cup toasted chopped walnuts and 1 teaspoon ground cinnamon to the batter.

Morning Glory Almond Waffles

These multigrain waffles are packed with healthful nutrients. In warm weather, fresh berries and yogurt make a delicious topping. When the weather is frosty, Sautéed Cinnamon Apple Slices are superb as a topping.

⅔ cup all-purpose flour

⅔ cup whole-wheat flour

½ cup oat or rye flour

6 tablespoons cornmeal or corn flour

⅔ cup toasted chopped almonds

¼ cup oat or wheat bran

2 teaspoons baking powder

½ teaspoon baking soda

¼ teaspoon salt

3 large eggs, separated

1 cup buttermilk

1 cup milk

¼ cup honey

¼ cup canola oil or unsalted butter, melted

Fresh sliced strawberries or blueberries and plain yogurt, Sautéed Cinnamon Apple Slices (page 83), or Almond-Honey Butter (page 75) for topping

Preheat a waffle iron. In a bowl, whisk together the flours, cornmeal, almonds, oat bran, baking powder, baking soda, and salt. In another bowl, beat the egg whites with an electric mixer until soft, glossy peaks form. In another bowl, beat or whisk together the egg yolks, buttermilk, milk, honey, and oil. Add the buttermilk mixture to the dry ingredients and mix just until combined. Fold in the egg whites.

Spoon or pour about 1 cup batter onto the hot iron. Close the lid. Bake until the waffle is golden brown, about 4 minutes. Remove with a fork to a warm plate. Serve at once or keep warm on a baking sheet in a 200°F oven. Repeat with the remaining batter. Top with berries and yogurt, Sautéed Cinnamon Apple Slices, or Almond-Honey Butter.

MAKES ABOUT 8 WAFFLES; SERVES 8

Variation:
Healthy Soy Waffles: Substitute ¼ cup soy flour for the ¼ cup oat bran. Serve with Sugar-Free Apple Spread (page 78).

Sweet-Spicy Buckwheat Waffles

A medley of spices and molasses complements buckwheat flour in these extra-crispy waffles. Buckwheat flour comes from the seeds of the buckwheat plant. It has a distinctive dark brown speckled color and a rich mineral and vitamin content.

1⅓ cups unbleached all-purpose flour

⅔ cup buckwheat flour

2 tablespoons packed dark brown sugar

2 teaspoons baking powder

2 teaspoons ground cardamom

1 teaspoon ground cinnamon

½ teaspoon baking soda

¼ teaspoon ground cloves

¼ teaspoon salt

2 large eggs, separated

1¾ cups milk

¼ cup molasses

¼ cup canola oil

Butter and maple syrup, honey, or Sautéed Cinnamon Apple Slices (page 83) for topping

Preheat a waffle iron. In a bowl, whisk together the flours, sugar, baking powder, cardamom, cinnamon, baking soda, cloves, and salt. In a small, deep bowl, beat the egg whites with an electric mixer until soft, glossy peaks form. In another bowl, beat or whisk together the egg yolks, milk, molasses, and oil. Add the milk mixture to the dry ingredients and mix just until combined. Fold in the egg whites.

Spoon or pour about 1 cup batter onto the hot iron. Close the lid. Bake until the waffle is golden brown, about 4 minutes. Remove with a fork to a warm plate. Serve at once or keep warm on a baking sheet in a 200°F oven. Repeat with the remaining batter. Top each waffle with butter and maple syrup, honey, or Sautéed Cinnamon Apple Slices.

MAKES ABOUT 6 WAFFLES; SERVES 6

Five-Grain Fitness Waffles

A variety of grains produces an intriguingly wholesome flavor in these tender-crisp waffles. You may purchase the various flours from bulk bins and can often zero in on organic flours. Accompany with maple syrup or whipped honey butter and partner with a fresh fruit salad for a healthful way to start the day.

⅔ cup all-purpose flour

½ cup whole-wheat flour

¼ cup barley flour

¼ cup corn flour or cornmeal

¼ cup rye flour

¼ cup buckwheat flour

¼ cup toasted wheat germ

2 teaspoons baking powder

1 teaspoon ground cardamom

½ teaspoon baking soda

¼ teaspoon salt

4 large eggs, separated

2 cups buttermilk

¼ cup canola oil or unsalted butter, melted

2 tablespoons honey or maple syrup

Maple syrup, Blueberry Sauce (page 79), or Swiss Whipped Honey Butter (page 74) for topping

Preheat a waffle iron. In a bowl, whisk together the flours, wheat germ, baking powder, cardamom, baking soda, and salt. In another bowl, beat the egg whites with an electric mixer until soft, glossy peaks form. In another bowl, beat or whisk together the egg yolks, buttermilk, oil, and honey. Add the buttermilk mixture to the dry ingredients and mix just until combined. Fold in the egg whites.

Spoon or pour about 1 cup batter onto the hot iron. Close the lid. Bake until the waffle is golden brown, about 4 minutes. Remove with a fork to a warm plate. Serve at once or keep warm on a baking sheet in a 200°F oven. Repeat with the remaining batter. Top with maple syrup, Blueberry Sauce, or Swiss Whipped Honey Butter.

MAKES ABOUT 8 WAFFLES; SERVES 8

Sesame Seed Multigrain Waffles

Toasted sesame seeds impart a snappy crunch to these flavorful waffles. A nutmeg grater is easy to use and it produces a fresher, premium flavor from whole nutmeg rather than using the preground spice.

1¼ cups whole-wheat pastry flour or all-purpose whole-wheat flour

½ cup unbleached all-purpose flour

½ cup cornmeal

½ cup toasted sesame seeds

¼ cup oat bran

2 teaspoons baking powder

½ teaspoon baking soda

½ teaspoon freshly grated nutmeg

¼ teaspoon salt

2 large eggs, separated

1½ cups buttermilk or plain yogurt

½ cup milk

4 tablespoons (½ stick) unsalted butter, melted, or canola oil

Maple syrup, fruit syrup, or honey for topping

Preheat a waffle iron. In a bowl, whisk together the flours, cornmeal, sesame seeds, oat bran, baking powder, baking soda, nutmeg, and salt. In a small, deep bowl, beat the egg whites with an electric mixer until soft, glossy peaks form. In another bowl, beat or whisk together the egg yolks, buttermilk, milk, and butter. Add the buttermilk mixture to the dry ingredients and mix just until combined. Fold in the egg whites.

Spoon or pour about 1 cup batter onto the hot iron. Close the lid. Bake until the waffle is golden brown, about 4 minutes. Remove with a fork to a warm plate. Serve at once or keep warm on a baking sheet in a 200°F oven. Repeat with the remaining batter. Top each waffle with maple syrup, fruit syrup, or honey.

MAKES ABOUT 8 WAFFLES; SERVES 8

Dried Cherry–Pistachio Cornmeal Waffles

Bedecked in red and green fruit and nuts, these crispy golden waffles are fun to serve at brunch during the holiday season. They are great topped with Swiss Whipped Honey Butter or Sugar-Free Apple Spread.

1½ cups unbleached all-purpose flour

½ cup cornmeal

½ cup dried cherries or dried cranberries

½ cup roasted unsalted pistachios

3 tablespoons packed light brown sugar

2 teaspoons baking powder

½ teaspoon baking soda

½ teaspoon salt

3 large eggs, separated

1 cup plain yogurt

1 cup milk

4 tablespoons (½ stick) unsalted butter, melted, or canola oil

Swiss Whipped Honey Butter (page 74) or Sugar-Free Apple Spread (page 78) for topping

Preheat a waffle iron. In a bowl, whisk together the flour, cornmeal, cherries, pistachios, sugar, baking powder, baking soda, and salt. In a small, deep bowl, beat the egg whites with an electric mixer until soft, glossy peaks form. In another bowl, beat or whisk together the egg yolks, yogurt, milk, and butter. Add the yogurt mixture to the dry ingredients and mix just until combined. Fold in the egg whites.

Spoon or pour about 1 cup batter onto the hot iron. Close the lid. Bake until the waffle is golden brown, about 4 minutes. Remove with a fork to a warm plate. Serve at once or keep warm on a baking sheet in a 200°F oven. Repeat with the remaining batter. Top with Swiss Whipped Honey Butter or Sugar-Free Apple Spread.

MAKES ABOUT 8 WAFFLES; SERVES 8

Tuscan Waffles

Fresh basil and pine nuts enhance these crispy waffles. These are good-looking topped with an olive tapenade and crème fraîche or sour cream for a special luncheon.

1½ cups all-purpose flour

⅔ cup garbanzo or chestnut flour

2 teaspoons baking powder

½ teaspoon baking soda

¼ teaspoon salt

2 large eggs, separated

1½ cups buttermilk

½ cup milk

¼ cup olive oil

½ cup pine nuts or chopped unsalted pistachios

¼ cup chopped fresh basil, plus extra for garnish

Tapenade (page 86), crème fraîche, or sour cream for topping

Preheat a waffle iron. In a bowl, whisk together the flours, baking powder, baking soda, and salt. In a small, deep bowl, beat the egg whites with an electric mixer until soft, glossy peaks form. In another bowl, beat or whisk together the egg yolks, buttermilk, milk, and oil. Add the buttermilk mixture, nuts, and basil to the dry ingredients and mix just until combined. Fold in the egg whites.

Spoon or pour about 1 cup batter onto the hot iron. Close the lid. Bake until the waffle is golden brown, about 4 minutes. Remove with a fork to a warm plate. Serve at once or keep warm on a baking sheet in a 200°F oven. Repeat with the remaining batter. Top with a spoonful of Tapenade, crème fraîche, or sour cream, and garnish with chopped basil.

MAKES ABOUT 6 WAFFLES; SERVES 6

Honey-Orange French Toast Waffles

Challah bread soaks in an orange-zested custard and then bakes in a waffle iron for a decorative shortcut to hot French toast. A country-style sweet French bread also works well here.

6 tablespoons orange juice concentrate

3 large eggs

3 tablespoons half-and-half or milk

1½ tablespoons unsalted butter, melted

1 tablespoon grated orange zest

1 tablespoon honey

8 to 10 slices challah or country-style bread, cut ½ inch thick

Honey, Homemade Maple Syrup (page 73), or Maple Sugar–Pecan Butter (page 74) for topping

Preheat a waffle iron. In a bowl, whisk together the orange juice concentrate, eggs, half-and-half, butter, zest, and honey. Soak the bread in the egg mixture for a few minutes on each side.

Place 1 or 2 slices at a time in the hot iron and close the lid. Bake until golden brown, about 3 minutes. Remove with a fork to a warm plate. Serve at once or keep warm on a baking sheet in a 200°F oven. Repeat with the remaining bread. Serve warm with honey, Homemade Maple Syrup, or Maple Sugar–Pecan Butter.

MAKES 8 TO 10 WAFFLE TOASTS; SERVES 4 TO 6

Cheddar Cheese–Chive Waffles

Top these sharp and tangy cheese waffles with salsa, your favorite chutney, or Sun-Dried Tomato Pesto for a savory brunch or lunch.

1½ cups unbleached all-purpose flour

½ cup rye flour

1 cup (4 ounces) grated sharp
  Cheddar cheese

⅓ cup minced fresh chives

2 teaspoons baking powder

½ teaspoon baking soda

½ teaspoon freshly grated nutmeg

¼ teaspoon salt

2 large eggs, separated

1½ cups buttermilk

½ cup milk

4 tablespoons (½ stick) unsalted butter, melted, or canola oil

Fruit Salsa (page 87), chutney, or
  Sun-Dried Tomato Pesto (page 85)
  for topping

Preheat a waffle iron. In a bowl, whisk together the flours, cheese, chives, baking powder, baking soda, nutmeg, and salt. In a small, deep bowl, beat the egg whites with an electric mixer until soft, glossy peaks form. In another bowl, beat or whisk together the egg yolks, buttermilk, milk, and butter. Add the buttermilk mixture to the dry ingredients and mix just until combined. Fold in the egg whites.

Spoon or pour about 1 cup batter onto the hot iron. Close the lid. Bake until the waffle is golden brown, about 4 minutes. Remove with a fork to a warm plate. Serve at once or keep warm on a baking sheet in a 200°F oven. Repeat with the remaining batter. Top each waffle with a spoonful of Fruit Salsa, chutney, or Sun-Dried Tomato Pesto.

MAKES ABOUT 8 WAFFLES; SERVES 8

Olive-Semolina Waffles

Semolina imparts a pale golden color and nutty flavor to these savory waffles. This flour is milled from hard durum wheat and is the basis of most pastas. Top these with Tapenade or Sun-Dried Tomato Pesto and a shower of basil and enjoy out of hand.

1 cup all-purpose flour

1 cup semolina flour

2 teaspoons baking powder

½ teaspoon baking soda

¼ teaspoon salt

2 large eggs, separated

1½ cups plain yogurt

½ cup milk

¼ cup olive oil

1½ cups chopped kalamata olives

Tapenade (page 86) or Sun-Dried
  Tomato Pesto (page 85) for topping

¼ cup chopped fresh basil for sprinkling

Preheat a waffle iron. In a bowl, whisk together the flours, baking powder, baking soda, and salt. In a small, deep bowl, beat the egg whites with an electric mixer until soft, glossy peaks form. In another bowl, beat or whisk together the egg yolks, yogurt, milk, and oil. Add the yogurt mixture and olives to the dry ingredients and mix just until combined. Fold in the egg whites.

Spoon or pour about 1 cup batter onto the hot iron. Close the lid. Bake until the waffle is golden brown, about 4 minutes. Remove with a fork to a warm plate. Serve at once or keep warm on a baking sheet in a 200°F oven. Repeat with the remaining batter. Top with a spoonful of Tapenade or Sun-Dried Tomato Pesto and sprinkle with basil.

MAKES ABOUT 8 WAFFLES; SERVES 8

Mocha Waffles with Chocolate Whipped Cream

The complementary duo of chocolate and coffee imparts a subtle mocha flavor to these elegant dessert waffles. They are sublime with the chocolate whipped cream and chocolate shavings, made by grating a bittersweet chocolate bar into fine shreds. As an alternative, top with coffee ice cream and hot fudge sauce.

CHOCOLATE WHIPPED CREAM
¾ cup heavy cream

3 tablespoons unsweetened cocoa powder

3 tablespoons sugar

2 tablespoons orange liqueur or dark rum

WAFFLES
2 cups all-purpose flour

⅔ cup packed brown sugar

½ cup unsweetened cocoa powder

2 teaspoons baking powder

½ teaspoon baking soda

¼ teaspoon salt

6 ounces bittersweet chocolate, plus extra for grating

½ cup strong coffee

6 tablespoons (¾ stick) unsalted butter

6 tablespoons espresso powder

4 large eggs, separated

1½ cups milk

To make the Chocolate Whipped Cream: In a bowl, whip the cream until soft peaks form and beat in the cocoa, sugar, and liqueur. Cover and refrigerate until needed or up to 2 days. This recipe yields about 1½ cups of whipped cream.

To make the waffles: Preheat a waffle iron. In a bowl, whisk together the flour, sugar, cocoa, baking powder, baking soda, and salt. In a small pan over simmering water, combine the chocolate, coffee, butter, and espresso powder, and stir until melted and blended. In another bowl, beat the egg whites with an electric mixer until soft, glossy peaks form. In another bowl, beat or whisk together the egg yolks, milk, and chocolate mixture. Add the milk mixture to the dry ingredients and mix just until combined. Fold in the egg whites.

(continued)

Spoon or pour about 1 cup batter onto the hot iron. Close the lid. Bake until the waffle is crisp, about 4 minutes. Remove with a fork to a warm plate. Serve at once or keep warm on a baking sheet in a 200°F oven. Repeat with the remaining batter. Top each waffle with a spoonful of Chocolate Whipped Cream and grate some chocolate over the top.

MAKES ABOUT 8 WAFFLES; SERVES 8

Lemon Zest Waffles with Raspberries and Crème Fraîche

A valuable tool for zesting citrus is the rasp-style grater, which is about 14 inches long and 1½ inches wide. With it placed across a bowl, you can achieve lots of fluffy zest in less than a minute as it yields far more zest than with the old-fashioned grater.

2 cups unbleached all-purpose flour

½ cup sugar

2 teaspoons baking powder

½ teaspoon baking soda

¼ teaspoon salt

3 large eggs, separated

1½ cups buttermilk

6 tablespoons freshly squeezed lemon juice

4 tablespoons (½ stick) unsalted butter, melted, or canola oil

2 tablespoons grated lemon zest

Fresh raspberries and crème fraîche or Raspberry-Framboise Sauce (page 82) for topping

Preheat a waffle iron. In a bowl, whisk together the flour, sugar, baking powder, baking soda, and salt. In another bowl, beat the egg whites with an electric mixer until soft, glossy peaks form. In another bowl, beat or whisk together the egg yolks, buttermilk, juice, butter, and zest. Add the buttermilk mixture to the dry ingredients and mix just until combined. Fold in the egg whites.

Spoon or pour about 1 cup batter onto the hot iron. Close the lid. Bake until the waffle is golden brown, about 4 minutes. Remove with a fork to a warm plate. Serve at once or keep warm on a baking sheet in a 200°F oven. Repeat with the remaining batter. Serve topped with raspberries and crème fraîche or Raspberry-Framboise Sauce.

MAKES ABOUT 6 WAFFLES; SERVES 6

Coconut–Macadamia Nut Waffles with Tropical Fruit Mélange

Toasted coconut and crunchy macadamia nuts lend an elegant touch to these delectable waffles. Smother them with a colorful fruit medley of fresh pineapple, mango, and kiwi fruit.

2 cups unbleached all-purpose flour

⅔ cup toasted unsweetened coconut

⅔ cup chopped macadamia nuts

3 tablespoons maple sugar or packed light brown sugar

2 teaspoons baking powder

½ teaspoon baking soda

1 teaspoon ground cardamom

¼ teaspoon salt

3 large eggs, separated

2 cups milk or coconut milk

4 tablespoons (½ stick) unsalted butter, melted, or canola oil

4 cups mixed diced fresh pineapple, mango or papaya, and kiwi fruit or Candied Ginger, Mango, and Lime Spread (page 77) for topping

Preheat a waffle iron. In a bowl, whisk together the flour, coconut, nuts, sugar, baking powder, baking soda, cardamom, and salt. In another bowl, beat the egg whites with an electric mixer until soft, glossy peaks form. In another bowl, beat or whisk together the egg yolks, milk, and butter. Add the milk mixture to the dry ingredients and mix just until combined. Fold in the egg whites.

Spoon or pour about 1 cup batter onto the hot iron. Close the lid. Bake until the waffle is golden brown, about 4 minutes. Remove with a fork to a warm plate. Serve at once or keep warm on a baking sheet in a 200°F oven. Repeat with the remaining batter. Serve topped with diced fresh fruit or Candied Ginger, Mango, and Lime Spread.

MAKES ABOUT 8 WAFFLES; SERVES 8

Belgian Chocolate Ice Cream Sundae Waffles

Dark chocolate waffles form a delectable cushion for an ice cream sundae. Pick your favorite frosty flavor—vanilla bean, coffee, or toasted almond are all good choices—to enrich this combination. The deep indentations of a Belgian waffle iron are ideal for holding the luscious sauce.

2 cups all-purpose flour

⅔ cup unsweetened cocoa powder

⅔ cup packed light brown sugar

2 teaspoons baking powder

½ teaspoon baking soda

Dash of salt

4 large eggs, separated

2 cups milk

6 tablespoons (¾ stick) unsalted butter, melted

2 teaspoons vanilla extract

1 quart vanilla bean, coffee, or toasted almond ice cream for topping

Rich Chocolate Sauce (page 89) or Raspberry-Framboise Sauce (page 82) for topping

Preheat a waffle iron. In a large bowl, whisk together the flour, cocoa, sugar, baking powder, baking soda, and salt. In another bowl, beat the egg whites with an electric mixer until stiff, glossy peaks form. In another bowl, beat or whisk together the egg yolks, milk, butter, and vanilla. Add the milk mixture to the dry ingredients and mix just until combined. Fold in the egg whites.

Spoon or pour about 1 cup batter onto the hot iron. Close the lid. Bake until the waffle is crisp, about 4 minutes. Remove with a fork to a warm plate. Serve at once or keep warm on a baking sheet in a 200°F oven. Repeat with the remaining batter. Top each warm waffle with a scoop of ice cream and a spoonful of Rich Chocolate Sauce or Raspberry-Framboise Sauce.

MAKES 6 TO 8 WAFFLES; SERVES 6 TO 8

Belgian Waffles with Berries and Whipped Cream

Honeycombed Belgian waffles make a dramatic cushion for a medley of strawberries, raspberries, and whipped cream. Most any waffle recipe works well in a Belgian waffle iron. This batter makes extra-crispy waffles.

2 cups all-purpose flour

1 tablespoon sugar

2½ teaspoons baking powder

¼ teaspoon salt

4 large eggs, separated

1½ cups milk

6 tablespoons (¾ stick) unsalted butter, melted, or canola oil

2 teaspoons vanilla extract

3 cups mixed fresh raspberries and sliced strawberries for topping

1 cup whipped cream, plain yogurt, or sour cream for topping

3 tablespoons raw sugar for topping

Preheat a Belgian waffle iron. In a bowl, whisk together the flour, sugar, baking powder, and salt. In another bowl, beat the egg whites with an electric mixer until soft, glossy peaks form. In another bowl, beat or whisk together the egg yolks, milk, butter, and vanilla. Add the milk mixture to the dry ingredients and mix just until combined. Fold in the egg whites.

Spoon or pour about 1 cup batter onto the hot iron. Close the lid. Bake until the waffle is golden brown, about 4 minutes. Remove with a fork to a warm plate. Serve at once or keep warm on a baking sheet in a 200°F oven. Repeat with the remaining batter. Top with berries, whipped cream, and raw sugar.

MAKES ABOUT 6 WAFFLES; SERVES 6

Red Pear–Almond Waffles

Nuggets of fresh pear and toasty almonds bejewel these crispy orange-scented waffles. Orange Butter Sauce is a superb accompaniment.

2 cups all-purpose flour

⅔ cup toasted chopped almonds

⅓ cup sugar

2 teaspoons baking powder

½ teaspoon baking soda

¼ teaspoon salt

4 large eggs, separated

1¼ cups milk

6 tablespoons (¾ stick) unsalted butter, melted, or canola oil

3 tablespoons orange juice concentrate

1 tablespoon grated orange zest

¼ teaspoon almond extract

1 large red Bartlett, Anjou, or Bosc pear, halved, cored, and finely chopped

Orange Butter Sauce (page 93) or Swiss Whipped Honey Butter (page 74) for topping

Preheat a waffle iron. In a bowl, whisk together the flour, almonds, sugar, baking powder, baking soda, and salt. In another bowl, beat the egg whites with an electric mixer until soft, glossy peaks form. In another bowl, beat or whisk together the egg yolks, milk, butter, orange juice concentrate, zest, and almond extract. Add the milk mixture to the dry ingredients and mix just until combined. Fold in the egg whites and pear.

Spoon or pour about 1 cup batter onto the hot iron. Close the lid. Bake until the waffle is golden brown, about 4 minutes. Remove with a fork to a warm plate. Serve at once or keep warm on a baking sheet in a 200°F oven. Repeat with the remaining batter. Top with Orange Butter Sauce or Swiss Whipped Honey Butter.

MAKES ABOUT 8 WAFFLES; SERVES 8

Chocolate-Hazelnut Waffles

Chocolate and hazelnuts are a winning duo in these crunchy dessert waffles that are delectable topped with fresh raspberries and crème fraîche or rich chocolate or caramel sauce.

2 cups all-purpose flour

4 ounces grated bittersweet chocolate

⅔ cup toasted chopped hazelnuts

⅓ cup sugar

2 teaspoons baking powder

½ teaspoon baking soda

¼ teaspoon salt

4 large eggs, separated

1½ cups milk

6 tablespoons (¾ stick) unsalted butter, melted, or canola oil

1 teaspoon vanilla extract

¼ teaspoon almond extract

2 cups fresh raspberries for topping

¾ cup crème fraîche or sour cream for topping

Preheat a waffle iron. In a bowl, whisk together the flour, chocolate, hazelnuts, sugar, baking powder, baking soda, and salt. In another bowl, beat the egg whites with an electric mixer until soft, glossy peaks form. In another bowl, beat or whisk together the egg yolks, milk, butter, vanilla, and almond extract. Add the milk mixture to the dry ingredients and mix just until combined. Fold in the egg whites.

Spoon or pour about 1 cup batter onto the hot iron. Close the lid. Bake until the waffle is golden brown, about 4 minutes. Remove with a fork to a warm plate. Serve at once or keep warm on a baking sheet in a 200°F oven. Repeat with the remaining batter. Top with raspberries and crème fraîche or sour cream.

MAKES ABOUT 8 WAFFLES; SERVES 8

Flavored Butters

This selection of flavored butters can be kept in the refrigerator ready for a last-minute topping.

SWISS WHIPPED HONEY BUTTER

⅔ cup honey

8 tablespoons (1 stick) unsalted butter
  at room temperature

½ cup heavy cream

In a small bowl, combine the honey and butter and beat with an electric mixer until light and fluffy. Add the cream and beat until blended. Spoon into a small bowl and serve or cover and refrigerate for up to 1 week.

MAKES ABOUT 1 ½ CUPS

MAPLE SUGAR–PECAN BUTTER

⅔ cup maple sugar or maple syrup

8 tablespoons (1 stick) unsalted butter
  at room temperature

½ cup toasted chopped pecans

In a small bowl, combine the maple sugar and butter and beat with an electric mixer until light and fluffy. Stir in the pecans. Spoon into a small bowl and serve or cover and refrigerate for up to 1 week.

MAKES ABOUT 1 ½ CUPS

ALMOND-HONEY BUTTER

⅔ cup honey

½ cup almond butter

4 tablespoons (½ stick) unsalted butter at room temperature

In a small bowl, combine the honey, almond butter, and butter and beat with an electric mixer until light and fluffy. Spoon into a small bowl and serve or cover and refrigerate for up to 1 week.

MAKES ABOUT 1¼ CUPS

Candied Ginger, Mango, and Lime Spread

Candied ginger and fresh lime heighten the flavor of this golden mango spread. It is a natural partner to Coconut-Macadamia Nut Waffles (page 66) or Ricotta Soufflé Pancakes (page 24).

2 large mangos (about 3 pounds), peeled, halved, and pitted

⅓ cup freshly squeezed lime juice

⅓ cup candied or crystallized ginger, thinly sliced

2 tablespoons honey

Freshly grated nutmeg (optional)

Preheat the oven to 300°F. Purée the mangos in a food processor with the juice, ginger, and honey. Place in a glass or non-aluminum baking dish and bake for 1 to 1¼ hours, stirring 2 or 3 times, or until reduced by half and thickened like a fruit butter. If desired, season to taste with nutmeg. Spoon into hot sterilized jars and seal. Let cool and refrigerate for up to 1 week.

MAKES ABOUT 3 CUPS

Sugar-Free Apple Spread

This spicy spread bakes to a caramelized golden hue and is superb on whole-grain pancakes, potato pancakes, and waffles. Various apple varieties will lend different flavors, varying from sweet to tart, so wait and add a touch of spice at the end of cooking. Tree-ripened Granny Smiths from a garden or open-air market lend an ideal sweet-tart ratio.

2 pounds apples, such as Granny Smith, Golden Delicious, Winesap, or Pippin, peeled and cored

One 6-ounce can apple juice concentrate, thawed

Ground cinnamon or mace

Preheat the oven to 300°F. Purée the apples in a food processor with the apple juice concentrate. Place in a glass or non-aluminum baking dish and bake for 1 hour, stirring 2 or 3 times, or until reduced by half and golden brown. Season to taste with cinnamon or mace. Spoon into hot sterilized jars and seal. Let cool and refrigerate for up to 1 week (or freeze for up to 3 months).

MAKES ABOUT 2 CUPS

Blueberry Sauce

This berry sauce is wonderful served warm over pancakes and waffles. Ladle it over Swedish Cinnamon-Rice Cakes (page 23) or Cottage Cheese Pancakes (page 26), or spoon it over Sesame Seed Multigrain Waffles (page 52) or Hazelnut-Orange Waffles (page 49).

⅓ cup sugar

1 tablespoon cornstarch

2 cups fresh or frozen blueberries

⅓ cup water

1½ teaspoons ground cinnamon

1 tablespoon freshly squeezed lemon juice

In a small saucepan, combine the sugar and cornstarch until evenly blended, then stir in the blueberries, water, and cinnamon. Bring to a boil over medium heat and simmer until slightly thickened. Remove from the heat and stir in the juice. Spoon into a heat-proof glass bowl and serve warm or cover and refrigerate for up to 1 week. Reheat in the microwave on medium power for 45 seconds or on the stove over low heat.

MAKES ABOUT 2 CUPS

Strawberry-Orange Sauce Flambé

For a gala flourish on dessert pancakes or waffles, flame this berry sauce at the table.

2 cups fresh or frozen halved strawberries

⅓ cup orange juice concentrate

¼ cup sugar

1 tablespoon freshly squeezed
  lemon juice

3 tablespoons orange liqueur

In a small saucepan, combine the strawberries, orange juice concentrate, sugar, and lemon juice. Bring to a boil and simmer for 2 minutes, or until heated through. Place in a heat-proof serving dish or spoon onto hot waffles or pancakes. Warm the liqueur in a small metal measuring cup over low heat, ignite it, and carefully spoon flaming liqueur over the berries. Serve at once.

MAKES ABOUT 2 CUPS

Raspberry-Framboise Sauce

This classic berry sauce is ideal cloaking strawberries and whipped cream on crisp Belgian waffles. Or spoon it over a trio of mixed berries—strawberries, blueberries, and raspberries—and vanilla bean ice cream for a delectable waffle dessert. It is also special paired with Ricotta Soufflé Pancakes (page 24) or Cottage Cheese Pancakes (page 26).

3 cups fresh raspberries

⅓ cup sugar

3 tablespoons freshly squeezed
  lemon juice

2 tablespoons framboise or other
  raspberry liqueur

Purée the raspberries in a blender and press them through a fine-mesh sieve into a bowl, discarding the seeds. Stir in the sugar, juice, and framboise. Serve immediately or cover and refrigerate for up to 1 week. Let warm to room temperature before serving.

MAKES ABOUT 2 CUPS

Sautéed Cinnamon Apple Slices

Granny Smith apples or other tart cooking apples caramelize to a delicious sweetness when sautéed in butter and sugar.

4 tablespoons (½ stick) unsalted butter at room temperature

4 large Granny Smith apples (about 1½ pounds), peeled, cored, and sliced

¼ cup sugar

1 teaspoon ground cinnamon or freshly grated nutmeg

In a 12-inch skillet over medium heat, melt the butter and add the apples. Sprinkle with sugar and cinnamon, and sauté, stirring, until soft and glazed, 8 to 10 minutes. Serve warm or reheat in a skillet over medium heat until heated through.

MAKES ABOUT 2 CUPS

Tapenade

This vibrant herb-scented olive spread is excellent over savory waffles and pancakes. Try it on Olive-Semolina Waffles (page 59) or Tuscan Waffles (page 54) along with a spoonful of Bulgarian yogurt or dollop of goat cheese.

One 6-ounce can pitted kalamata olives

½ cup unsalted pistachios or toasted walnuts

¼ cup fresh basil or minced fresh parsley

2 green onions, including tops, chopped

2 large cloves garlic, minced

2 tablespoons grated Parmesan cheese

3 or 4 strips lemon zest, minced

1 tablespoon freshly squeezed lemon juice

1 tablespoon balsamic vinegar

1 teaspoon Dijon mustard

2 tablespoons olive oil

Freshly ground black pepper

In a food processor fitted with the metal blade, blend the olives, pistachios, basil, onions, garlic, cheese, zest, juice, vinegar, and mustard until minced. Add the oil and blend in. Season with pepper to taste. Transfer to a bowl, cover, and refrigerate for up to 1 week.

MAKES ABOUT 1¼ CUPS

Fruit Salsa

This zesty salsa can be made with various fruits to uplift Coconut–Macadamia Nut Waffles (page 66) or Five-Grain Fitness Waffles (page 51).

2 cups diced peeled mango, papaya, peaches, or nectarines

½ cup diced red onion

½ cup diced red bell pepper or halved red seedless grapes

¼ cup chopped fresh cilantro

2 tablespoons freshly squeezed lime juice

2 teaspoons grated peeled fresh ginger

Dash of chili powder

In a medium bowl, combine the mango, onion, bell pepper, cilantro, juice, ginger, and chili powder. Mix lightly. Cover and chill until serving time.

MAKES ABOUT 3 CUPS

Rich Chocolate Sauce

This thick bittersweet chocolate sauce hardens as it coats frosty ice cream with a rich and shiny glaze for a sumptuous finish on sundae-style waffles or pancakes.

6 ounces bittersweet or semisweet chocolate, cut in chunks, or 1 cup chocolate chips

½ cup light cream or coffee

¼ cup light corn syrup

1 teaspoon vanilla extract

1 tablespoon brandy (optional)

In the top of a double boiler over simmering water, combine the chocolate, cream, and corn syrup, stirring until smooth. Stir in the vanilla and brandy, if desired. Transfer to a bowl and serve immediately or cover and refrigerate for up to 1 week. Reheat in a heat-proof container in the microwave on high heat for 30 seconds or over a pan of simmering water.

MAKES ABOUT 1 ⅓ CUPS

Butterscotch Sauce

For a festive waffle sundae, spoon this luscious brown sugar sauce over Belgian Chocolate Waffles (page 67), Coconut-Macadamia Nut Waffles (page 66), or Crêpes (page 36) rolled with vanilla bean or coffee ice cream.

1⅓ cups packed light brown sugar

⅔ cup light corn syrup

4 tablespoons (½ stick) unsalted butter at room temperature

Dash of salt

⅓ cup heavy cream

1 teaspoon vanilla extract

In a small saucepan, combine the sugar, corn syrup, butter, and salt, and cook over low heat, stirring occasionally, until the mixture has the consistency of heavy cream, about 5 minutes. Remove from heat and stir in the cream and vanilla. Transfer to a bowl and serve immediately or cover and refrigerate for up to 1 week. Reheat in a heat-proof container in the microwave on high heat for 30 seconds or over a pan of simmering water.

MAKES ABOUT 1½ CUPS

Caramel Sauce

Caramelizing sugar develops a rich flavor and deep brown color in this dessert sauce. The secret to avoiding crystallization is to swirl and shake the pan in the beginning until the sugar dissolves. Enjoy this sauce warm over dessert pancakes and waffles.

1 cup sugar

¼ cup water

4 tablespoons (½ stick) unsalted butter
  at room temperature

½ cup heavy cream

1 teaspoon vanilla extract

Place the sugar and water in a small saucepan over medium heat, shaking and swirling the pan without boiling until the sugar dissolves. Then bring to a boil, cover, and cook for 1 minute. Remove the cover and boil until the syrup develops a rich, dark color, 5 to 7 minutes. Remove from the heat, add the butter, stirring to melt, then stir in the cream and vanilla. Transfer to a bowl and serve warm or at room temperature. Or cover and refrigerate for up to 1 week. Reheat in a heat-proof container in the microwave on high heat for 30 seconds or over a pan of simmering water.

MAKES ABOUT 1 ½ CUPS

Rum Hard Sauce

This hard sauce laced with rum, brandy, amaretto, or vanilla makes for a special finish on pancakes or waffles. Though the sauce is basically soft and fluffy, the name stems from the hard alcohol that often flavors it as a traditional partner to English plum pudding.

12 tablespoons (1 ½ sticks) unsalted
  butter at room temperature

1 ½ cups confectioners' sugar

1 tablespoon rum, brandy, or amaretto
  or 1 teaspoon vanilla extract

Dash of salt

Freshly grated nutmeg

In a small bowl, beat the butter with an electric mixer until creamy. Sift the sugar and gradually add it to the butter, beating until blended. Stir in the rum and salt, beating until blended. Spoon into a bowl and top with the nutmeg. Serve immediately or cover and refrigerate for up to 1 week. Let warm slightly at room temperature before serving.

MAKES ABOUT 1 ¼ CUPS

Variation:
Apricot or Cherry Hard Sauce: Mix in ⅓ cup diced dried apricots or cherries with the rum and salt.

Orange Butter Sauce

This quick-to-prepare citrus sauce is delectable with a bit of orange liqueur—Cointreau, triple sec, or Grand Marnier—but it is also excellent unembellished. It enhances a variety of pancakes and waffles: Granola-Yogurt Pancakes (page 20), Swedish Cinnamon-Rice Cakes (page 23), Hazelnut-Orange Waffles (page 49), or Morning Glory Almond Wafffles (page 44).

One 6-ounce can orange juice concentrate

8 tablespoons (1 stick) unsalted butter at room temperature

¼ cup sugar

2 tablespoons Cointreau, Grand Marnier, or other orange liqueur (optional)

Combine the orange juice concentrate, butter, and sugar in a small saucepan and gently bring to a boil, stirring to dissolve the sugar. Stir in the liqueur, if desired. Serve warm or at room temperature. Or, cover and refrigerate for up to 1 week. Reheat in a heat-proof container in the microwave on high heat for 30 seconds or over a pan of simmering water.

MAKES ABOUT 1½ CUPS

INDEX

TABLE OF EQUIVALENTS

The exact equivalents in the following tables have been rounded for convenience.

LIQUID/DRY MEASURES

U.S.	METRIC
¼ teaspoon	1.25 milliliters
½ teaspoon	2.5 milliliters
1 teaspoon	5 milliliters
1 tablespoon (3 teaspoons)	15 milliliters
1 fluid ounce (2 tablespoons)	30 milliliters
¼ cup	60 milliliters
⅓ cup	80 milliliters
½ cup	120 milliliters
1 cup	240 milliliters
1 pint (2 cups)	480 milliliters
1 quart (4 cups, 32 ounces)	960 milliliters
1 gallon (4 quarts)	3.84 liters
1 ounce (by weight)	28 grams
1 pound	454 grams
2.2 pounds	1 kilogram

OVEN TEMPERATURE

FAHRENHEIT	CELSIUS	GAS
250	120	½
275	140	1
300	150	2
325	160	3
350	180	4
375	190	5
400	200	6
425	220	7
450	230	8
475	240	9
500	260	10

LENGTH

U.S.	METRIC
⅛ inch	3 millimeters
¼ inch	6 millimeters
½ inch	12 millimeters
1 inch	2.5 centimeters